Whispers of a One-Eyed Raven:
Mythological Poetry

Also by John W. Leys:
The Darkness of His Dreams: Poetry (2019)

Other books containing poetry by John W. Leys:
All the Lonely People by Nicholas Gagnier (2019)

Avalanches in Poetry: Poetry, Stories, and Art Inspired by Leonard Cohen, edited by David L. O'Nan (2019)

As the World Burns: Writers and Artists Reflect on a World Gone Mad, edited by Kindra M. Austin, Candice Louisa Daquin, Rachel Finch, and Christine E. Ray (2020)

Whispers of a One-Eyed Raven

Mythological Poetry

John W. Leys

Broken Wing Publishing
Albany, Oregon

Copyright © 2020 John W. Leys

All rights reserved. No part of this publication may be reproduced, distributed, or transmitted in any form by any means, including photocopying, recording, or other electronic methods without the prior written permission of the author, except in the case of brief quotations embodied in reviews and certain other noncommercial uses permitted by copyright law.

Many the poems in this collection first appeared, in earlier revisions, on http://johnwleys.com/

'At the Beginning…' first appeared in FreeVerse Revolution (https://freeverserevolution.wordpress.com)

'Twilight Visions' first appeared in The Ink Owl (https://inkowlme.wordpress.com)

Cover Design by John W. Leys

ISBN: (Paperback) 978-1-7333645-2-2
ISBN: (eBook) 978-1-7333645-3-9

Library of Congress Control Number: 2020919708

First Published: November 2020 by Broken Wing Publishing

Dedicated to
Edith Hamilton (1867-1963),
whose book *Mythology* introduced me to the world of
Myths nearly 40 years ago.

*"Blessed are the legend-makers with their rhyme
of things not found within recorded time.*

- J.R.R. Tolkien, *Mythopoeia* (1931)

*"…words and visions pass through my brain,
down my arm, and into my right hand,
As if whispered in my ear by a one-eyed raven
sitting on my shoulder
Telling me about his day."*

-John W. Leys, *The Darkness of His Dreams* (2019)

Contents

INTRODUCTION	**13**
MYTHS AND LEGENDS	13
MYTHOPOEIA	16
THE POEMS	19
NOTES ON PRONUNCIATION	**21**
NON-ENGLISH CHARACTERS	21
OLD NORSE	21
WELSH PRONUNCIATION	23
GAELIC PRONUNCIATIONS	25
WHISPERS OF A ONE-EYED RAVEN	**27**
AT THE BEGINNING...	**31**
RECOLLECTIONS AND WARNINGS	**34**
I.	34
II.	37
III.	39
IV	41
V.	44
VI.	47
NÍU HEIMAR	**49**
YGGDRASIL	**52**
WODANAZ	**53**
HIGH, JUST AS HIGH; THIRD (TANKA)	**54**
HUGINN AND MUNINN (HAIKU)	**55**
THE PROMISE OF THE RUNES	**56**
MOTHER FRIGG	**57**

ÞÓRR	58
MJÖLNIR (HAIKU)	59
LOKI, OÐINN BROTHER	60
TYR	61
ÓÐRŒRIR (A TANKA)	62
STARING INTO THE FLAMES.	63
WINTER SOLSTICE WILD HUNT	64
BURROWERS IN THE DEEP	66
RAGNARÖK	68
WARS IN HEAVEN	70
I. URANUS AND KRONOS	70
II. KRONOS AND ZEUS	72
SHADOW AND LIGHT	75
OF ALFAR AND DVERGAR	76
MOTHER DANU	79
BLESSED BRAN	81
THE RAVEN, THE EAGLE, AND THE RED DRAGON	82
THE DRAGONS OF DINAS EMRYS	85
MERLIN	88
A SONG OF TALIESIN	89
EXCERPT FROM THE TALE OF MYRDDIN WYLLT	95
I. THE AFTERMATH OF ARFDERYDD	95
II. MYRDDIN'S SONG	97
III. MYRDDIN'S LAMENT	99
IV. GWENDYDD'S SONG	101

UNDER THE SÍDHE	**103**
TWILIGHT VISIONS	**106**
APPENDIX I: PRONUNCIATION GUIDE	**109**
APPENDIX II: SUGGESTED FURTHER READING	**138**
General Mythology	138
Norse Mythology:	138
Celtic Mythology (Including Arthurian Legends)	139
Classical Mythology	141
ACKNOWLEDGMENTS	**142**
ABOUT THE AUTHOR	**144**

Introduction

Myths and Legends

In modern colloquial parlance, the word *myth* is used to denote an untruth, misconception, or an outright lie. This has colored many people's conception of what is meant when one speaks of a *myth* or *mythology*.

Our word *myth* comes directly from the ancient Greek word μῦθος (mȳthos), which was used by poets, such as Homer and his contemporaries, to evoke several related meanings, including 'narrative,' 'conversation,' 'story,' 'tale,' or 'word.' Notably, the term doesn't distinguish between true and false stories, tales, or narratives. Μῦθος was combined with the suffix -λογία (-logia, 'study') to create the word μυθολογία (mythología), which was used to denote the act of storytelling. Socrates' student Plato would use the term to refer to any form of storytelling, whether it be "true" or not.

Μυθολογία was then borrowed into Late Latin by Fabius Planciades Fulgentius in his work *Mythologiæ*, where it is used to denote what we now refer to as 'Classical Mythology,' that is the traditional Greco-Roman etiological stories of their gods and tales of their heroes. Of note is the fact that Fulgentius is careful to refer to these stories as purely allegorical tales to be interpreted and not a record of true events, a view perhaps informed by his Christian faith.

By the early 19th Century myth had been adopted by scholars as a technical term denoting a "traditional story, especially one concerning the early history of a people or explaining a natural or social phenomenon, and typically involving supernatural beings or events."[1] When I was studying for my BA in Religious Studies, the short and simple definition of *myth* was "a sacred story," with the caveat that many only refer to other people's sacred stories as "myths," since the notion that myth=falsehood is so deeply ingrained in the modern mind.

Closely related to myth is the term *legend*, which is usually differentiated from *myth* by being based on actual historical events and being centered around human beings rather that supernatural spirits or deities (i.e. the Legend of King Arthur). Hippolyte Delehaye drew the line between *myth* and *legend* as such, "The legend, on the other hand, has, of necessity, some historical or topographical connection. It refers imaginary events to some real personage, or it localizes romantic stories in some definite spot."[2] Which is all good and fine, but the stories themselves refuse to fit into our handy categories. To wit, the story of the Trojan War as

---

[1] "mythos, n." 2003. In Oxford English Dictionary (3rd ed.). Oxford: Oxford University Press.

[2] Hippolyte Delehaye, The Legends of the Saints: An Introduction to Hagiography (1907), Chapter I: Preliminary Definitions.

recorded by Homer in the *Illiad* and the *Odyssey* is generally regarded to be a part of the Greek mythological corpus, however, it is based around actual historical events and is focused on human beings—though the Olympian Gods do play major roles themselves. One could argue for its inclusion under either term, but other than a pedantic obsession with categorization, I'm not sure what the point would be.

In its original English usage, *legend* referred to a narrative of events. Later, in the 17th Century, it started being used by English speaking Protestants to indicate that an event (usually the tale of any Saint not recognized by *Foxe's Book of Martyrs*) was fictitious, with the "true narratives" being reserved for *chronicles*. And to this day to call something a "legend" is to imply that it is at least partially a lie.

But Myths and Legends are not lies. As Neil Gaiman, once wrote in his *Sandman* comic book series:

> *"Things need not have happened to be true. Tales and dreams are the shadow-truths that will endure when mere facts are dust and ashes, and forgot."*[3]

Myths are stories without authors, composed before we wrote things down, when everything was recorded

---

[3] Gaiman, Neil. Sandman #19. Page 21, Panel 5. DC Comics 1990

on the poet's tongue and in the bard's breath. Homer, Virgil and the rest were recorders, reinterpreters; embellishers of myths, not the creators of myths. These stories stem from a time when the border between dream and reality was barely drawn, when the wall between this world and the other was but a thin membrane, at best. They were our first attempt to make sense of the world around us, using inspiration and imagination, before the philosophers invented epistemology and the scientific method. They are stories that hold truths that linger in the darkened hallways and under the hollow hills, that enchant the imagination and stir the poet's heart.

Mythopoeia

The word *mythopoeia* (sometimes given as *mythopoesis*[4]) derives from the Ancient Greek μυθοποιία (or μυθοποίησις), which literally means "myth-making," and until relatively recent times it referred to the creation of myths in ancient times. J.R.R. Tolkien used the term as the title of a 1931 poem in which he defended mythology and the creative art of myth-making. At that time Tolkien had already been hard at work creating his own mythology for many years. The poem was prompted by a conversation between himself and good friend C.S. Lewis who had said that myths were "lies breathed through silver," meaning that they were pretty, yet worthless. Tolkien took very

---

[4] Interestingly, the second part of this word, poesis (ποίησις), which denotes the act of creation, is derived from the Greek verb ποιέω (poiéō), which means "to make," from which we also derive the word *poetry*.

much the opposite view, feeling that myths and "fairy stories" contained many elemental truths, and that the act of myth-making could help unearth and express these truths.

Since then mythopoeia has come to be used as a genre of fiction in which the author endeavors to create their own mythology. Tolkien's works, specifically the *Silmarillion,* are— aside from the poetry of William Blake—possibly the best example of such an invented mythology in which aspects and themes of real-world mythologies are taken as inspiration and molded into something new which incorporates the truths the author wishes to explore, mimicking the evolution of myth from oral to written traditions.

The reason I bring up this concept of mythmaking is because several of the poems (or parts thereof) in this collection have their origin in, or have been influenced by, my own mythopoesis. Around 25 years ago, when the seeds of this collection were being sown, I had become obsessed with the legends of King Arthur and readily devoured every version and variation of the Arthurian cycle that I could get my hands on. During this immersion in Arthuriana, I toyed with the idea of writing my own "definitive" version of the legend, hewing as close as possible to actual history and incorporating as much of the earliest traditions, which I saw as being the most "authentic," as possible. While formulating this project I happened upon Geoffrey of Monmouth's *Historia Regum Britanniae*[5], which contains the earliest extant complete Arthurian narrative. It also contains a fanciful history of Britain that traces its line of kings back to the Trojan War. I immediately fell in love with this medieval pseudo-history. As actual history Geoffrey's work is very nearly worthless, but as a creative work, as a work of mythopoesis, it is groundbreaking. Just as Tolkien had wanted to create a great mythology for England, so Geoffrey had wanted to create a great history for Britain to rival that of Rome, which was still the standard bearer of "civilization." He combined history with legends, myths, and his own imagination to create an epic tale that starts, as did Livy's *History of Rome*, with Aeneas fleeing from the burning Troy and ends nearly 1900 years later with the death of Cadwaladr and the final takeover of Britain by the Saxons.

My goal then became to write my own version of Geoffrey's *Historia*, making it conform more closely to known history. This resulted in a deep dive into ancient British and Roman history, legends, and mythology. To say that the tale "grew in the telling" would be a massive understatement, though relatively little of it has, as of yet, actually been written, existing only in notes, charts, timelines, and images in my imagination. None of this mythopoesis of mine has been seen publicly, save for a short piece posted on

---

[5] The History of the Kings of Britain. It was originally titled *De gestis Britonum* (*On the Deeds of the Britons*)

my blog a few years ago, until now.

The Poems
The bulk of the poems in this collection are based on or inspired by the myths of the Norse and the Celts, with one foray into Classical Mythology[6]. Some are retellings of old stories, some reference lesser known alternate versions of these famous myths, some are speculative, some are meditative, and some are linguistic jazz. Only one is purely extracted from my own mythopoesis, though aspects of this untold tale are sprinkled throughout the poems collected here.

These poems were largely written for my own amusement, with no inkling that anyone other than myself would be entertained by them. Much to my surprise, early versions of these poems received incredibly positive feedback on my blog, so much so that a dedicated collection seemed like a good idea.

This collection is very much a passion project for me, which I have referred to only partially jokingly as my "concept album." It is a rather huge departure from my first collection of poetry, but one I feel I needed to make. I have lived with, and within, these myths for a very long time, and in a very real way they will always be a part of me. This collection is my way of sharing that part of myself with all of you. Thank you

---

[6] Well, two forays, if you count the heavy borrowing from the Orphic creation myths in the opening poem.

for coming on this journey with me, I hope you enjoy it!

-John W. Leys
Albany, Oregon
4 October 2020

Notes on Pronunciation

Within the poems in this collection I have endeavored to, for the sake of authenticity, where possible, to use the un-anglicized forms of proper names that originally appeared in other languages. As a result, there are many words and names appearing in this book that the reader may need help in pronouncing. For help with pronouncing specific names, I refer the reader to *Appendix I*.

Non-English Characters

Below are a couple non-standard letters, generally not found in modern English, that appear in several names in the text, usually in older, sometimes hypothetical, (Proto) Indo-European names.[7]

β – Pronounced as "v" This is actually the Greek letter Beta, which is used in the International Phonetic Alphabet to represent the "voiced bilabial fricative."

3 / ȝ – Yogh. Pronounced as the "y" in youth.

Old Norse

Old Norse is a Germanic language, so many of the letters are pronounced the same as in English, with a

---

[7] To be honest, I could have written these names with the standard Roman Alphabet, but felt that these non-standard letters lent a wonderful air of foreign ancientness to the names.

few notable exceptions:

Æ / æ – Pronounced as the "a" in Days.
Ð / ð – Eth. Pronounced as the "th" in That.
F – (Initial) Pronounced as in far. (Middle or Final position) Pronounced as in very.
G – (Initial, after n) Pronounced as in good. (Before s or t) Pronounced as "ch" in loch
J – Pronounced as "y"
K – Pronounced as the "c" in call, unless immediately preceding "s" or "t" when pronounced as "ch" in loch.
L – Voiceless directly after "h" at the beginning of a word, ends of words after voiceless consonants or between voiceless consonants.
P – Pronounced as in English, unless preceding "s" or "t" when it is pronounced like the "f" in far.
Q – Pronounced as the "c" in call.
R – Trilled / Rolled.
Þ / þ – Thorn. Pronounced as the "th" in Thor.
X – Pronounced as the "chs" in lochs.
Z – pronounced like the "ts" in cats (as in German).

In Old Norse names there is often a final consonant that appears unpronounced in the transliterations. This can cause some confusion as *Freyr* is pronounced "Frey" yet *Baldr* is pronounced "Bald-er." For specific pronunciations I, again, refer the reader to *Appendix I*.

These are very basic rules, for more information I suggest the following webpage:

https://en.wikibooks.org/wiki/Old_Norse/Grammar/Alphabet_and_Pronunciation

Welsh Pronunciation
Welsh can be a tricky language to pronounce for non-native speakers. The following should help for the purposes of this book:

Consonants
C – Pronounced as in cat, never as in center
Ch – Pronounced as in the Scottish loch, or the German Bach; not as in church.
DD – Pronounced as the "th" in That.
F – Pronounced as "v"
FF – Pronounced as "f"
G – Pronounced as in get, never as in gem.
LL – Pronounced by placing your tongue behind your front teeth, as though you were going to pronounce an L, and then blow. There is no English equivalent.
NG – Pronounced as the "ng" in long.
PH – Pronounced as in phone.
R – Trilled /Rolled.
RH – Pronounced the same as R while blowing (Similar to LL)
S – Pronounced as in bus, never as in laser.
TH – Pronounced as in bath.

Vowels

Short

- **A** – Pronounced as in pat
- **E** – Pronounced as in pet
- **I** – Pronounced as in pit
- **O** – Pronounced as in pot
- **U** – Pronounced as the "I" in pit.
- **W** – Pronounced as the "oo" in book.
- **Y** – Pronounced as the "u" in cut, unless used in the last syllable of a word, then as the "ee" in beet.

Long

- **A** – Pronounced as in father
- **E** – Pronounced as the "ea" in bear
- **I** – Pronounced as in machine
- **O** – Pronounced as the "aw" in hawk
- **U** – Pronounced as "i" in machine.
- **W** – Pronounced as the "oo" in pool.
- **Y** – Pronounced as the "i" machine.

Welsh words tend to be stressed on the penultimate syllable, i.e. Rhiannon is pronounced RhiANNon, Carmarthen is pronounced CarMARthen, Meredith is pronounced MerEDith.

These are very basic rules, for more information I suggest the following webpage:
https://en.wikibooks.org/wiki/Welsh/Pronunciation

Gaelic Pronunciations

Irish Gaelic is even more complicated to pronounce than Welsh. In the interest of saving time and space, and since there are relatively few Irish Gaelic names/word in this book, I refer the reader to Appendix I: The Glossary and Pronunciation Guide, where I provide pronunciations for the specific names used within the text.

For those wanting an in-depth explanation of Irish Gaelic pronunciation, I recommend this webpage: https://en.wikibooks.org/wiki/Irish/Reference/Pronunciation

Whispers of a One-Eyed Raven

Sing to me, O Muses
The sacred songs
History holds so dear,
Calliope, Euterpe; Polyhymnia,
Daughters of Zeus I ask
For three drops of Awen,
Spilled from Ceridwen's cauldron,
Just a taste of Oðinn's
Sweet sacred mead,
So my brow will shine
As I sing my songs
Like a madman
In Celyddon's Wood.

At the Beginning...

For unknown æons
In the timeless halls
Of the gaping void
There was nothing.
Nothing was born,
Nothing existed,
Nothing lived,
Nothing aged,
And, finally,
Nothing died.

Inevitably,
Given innumerable time,
Out of necessity,
From nothing,
Something happened.
Something was born,
Something lived;
Something would
Never die.

A seed planted
In Darkness,
An egg laid in the night.
Embryonic everything
Incubating within
Its silver shell,
Cradled in
The chaos chasm,
Warmed by
The amniotic waters
Of Okeanus'
Dark depths.

Everything
Within that shell
Evolving,
Everything expanding,
Silver shell cracking,
Exploding unbridled
Undying light.

Escaping
In stars captured,
Burning,
In constellations collected,
Coalescing,
In milky white roads,
Against the darkness,
Universe birthing.

Entropy ordered
By unseen hands,
Dragons and demons,
Angels and eagles,
Orcs and elves,
Fire and ice,
Enduring earth
Separated from
Shining sky,
The world made right.
Monsters slaughtered
Mountains carved
From their thighs.

Mud and clay
molded.
Ash and elm wood
whittled.
Stones over the shoulder
thrown.
Order imposed.

The wyrd of the world
Lies in the garden
Where the sacred
Tree grows.

Recollections and Warnings

I.

Listen and attend
Sons and daughters
Of Ash and Elm,
Grandchildren of Yggdrasil,
To the visions and memories
I share and recite!
Older than all your
Gods and kings
am I,
More ancient than
All your cities
And all your petty borders.

I recall when Alßiz's kin
First arrived in moonlight
Along the banks of the Rhun,
Long before the sons of Ðanuz
Founded the cities of the north,
Or a single tunnel dug,
By the sons of Ðwerȝaz,
Into the depths below
Niðavellir's dark fields.

I observed when Æliz
Took up his holy misguided mission,
Departing for the east,
Where Anþaraz fled.
When βurista still stood,
Before brother βanðr fell
Into darkness and chaos.

Generations before the tyranny
Of Ymir, gluttonous great-grandson
Of Þurisaz the bold,
Who brought with him
The Long Winter of Aurgelmir
From which only Woðanaz
And the sons of Borr could thaw
And restore Order to the world,

Darkness returned to Alfgarð
A broken brother
Seeking converts
To his lies.
Scales thrown out of balance,
Chaos and fire
Ruled the night.
Durinn forged
A sacred sword of light
For the king to cut
The darkness from his doom,
Ignoring Alβ3uz's warning
That from the brightest flame
Is the darkest shadow cast.

The battle won,
The garden burnt,
The Álfarfoðr lay dead,
Brother's blood staining
His battered blade.

The bones of their brethren
Still smoking,
Their gleaming towers
Burnt to ash,
The fair folk in mourning
Turned northward
In search of
Whatever future they had.

A fall and a long winter later,
When your memories
Had barely begun,
I witnessed
The Alföðr and his brothers
Raise walls made
Of Jotnar bones,
To protect the saplings
Of Ash and Elm
From the chaos and wrath
Of the insatiable offspring
of Ymir's loins,
In the garden at the heart
Of the world.

II.
Behind these sacred walls,
Sowing your gardens,
Nursing your babes,
And fighting your petty squabbles,
What know ye
Of the world beyond,
And the wyrd
That worries the One-Eyed?

What do you know
Of the wars of gods and elves,
Of treason and treaties,
And guests burned black?

What do you know
Of Ásgarð's walls,
Of Loki's brood,
And Jotnar ground up
By a thunderclap?

Of shaved heads,
Of golden wigs,
And godly treasures
By Dvergar hand devised?

Of folding ships,
Short-handled hammers,
And devious
Biting flies?

What do you know
Of poetry's mead,
Of Mimir's head,
And the three maids
Who came from the east?

What do you know
Of Oðinn's sacrifice,
Of his missing eye,
And what doom
He prepares to meet?

III.
It begins
When mischief turns
To maleficence,
When the bold prince
Is murdered by mistletoe
Loosed from the hand of Hoðr,
Aimed by Loki's eye.

In Fensalir, Frigg's tears fall,
While vengeance rings out
From Valhalla:
Rindr's son rides out,
A day after being born,
To dispatch Hoðr to Hel.

The Trickster is taken
And Vali in wolf-coat
Slaughters the Lie Smith's son,
Using his bowels to bind
The Alfoðr's blood-brother
To a table of stone,
While venom drips
Into his eyes
From Skaði's snake,
Unless Sigyn can
Catch it first.

There follows
Three winters
Each colder than the last.
Each Summer shorter,
Each Fall faster
Until the sun turns black.

Then comes the Fimbulvetr,
The Great Winter,
Sol will sail
Her course thrice,
Though no summer is seen.

The bonds of brotherhood
Are broken
By desire and greed,
Blood spilled on blades
Of axes and swords.

The Hanged One's hall
Swells with new recruits:
The fallen warriors
From the fields of men.
The Valkyrie-chosen,
The Grey Beard's
Golden game pieces.

Fodder for the Jotunn
And Surtr's children
When the doom
At twilight comes.

IV
The Great Winter continues,
Cocks crow
From the heavens
Above Valhalla
To the cold halls
Of Eljuðnir
In the dark depths
Of the mansions of Hel.

Chains crack,
Loosing the wolves:
Garm the guard
At Niflhel's gates;
Fenrisulfr
By Gleipnir bound,
Through Æsir fear
A taste for divine blood
He developed.

In the iron woods
Of Jarnviðr,
Where Fenrir's brood
By Angrboða
Were bred:
Skoll, Sol swollower,
Hati, Mani murderer,
And their brethren,
A howling hoard of hounds
Ready to wreak havoc
On the worlds
Of gods and men.

The world wyrm writhes;
Waves wreck the beaches.
Miðgarð farms flood;
Dwarrow mines drown
As Þorr's bane prepares
For battle.

The bound god
Breaks his bonds
To captain the ship
Built of dead men's nails,
Riding the waves
Of Jormungandr's rage,
Sailing where destiny calls.

On the fields of Vigriðr
Assemble the adversaries
Of Æsir, Alfar, and Men:
Wyrm and wolves,
Sons of Surtr,
Jotnar of Hrym from the east.

The High One knows
What the ravens tell,
And can see
With his own keen eye.
The day has come,
Long foretold
When all the gods
Will die.

Heimdallr blows
The Gjallarhorn,
Which was dipped
In wisdom's well
In days long gone by.

The note is heard
Across nine worlds,
Shaking the world trees roots.
The Æsir awake
For one last þing
Before they meet
Their fate.

V.
The gods of Asgarð
Gather at the edge
Of the fields of Vigriðr,
One hundred leagues
From Hel's host,
Golden helmeted
Grimnir,
Dvergr forged Gungnir
In hand,
Riding eight legged
Sleipnir,
Loki's only faithful child,
At the lead.

The stars fall
As the sky is torn asunder
Revealing the flames
Of Muspelheim.
Surtr's shining sword
Strikes down
Alfheim's king,
Setting fire to the land.
The sons of Muspel
Advance on Asgarð,
Battering the Bifrost
Shattering
The shimmering bridge,
Burning
Great mansions
And hallowed halls,
Melting
The thirteen golden thrones
Of Glaðsheimr,

Leaving nothing
On Iðavollr's plain
But ash and dust.

Frigg's tears flow
Once more,
As Woden is taken
By the wolf
Who took Tyr's hand.

Viðarr Alfoðr-son
Pierces Fenrir's heart,
Avenging foul death,
Though the One-Eye
Will never more be seen.

Thunder slaughters
The treacherous serpent
With a mighty
Mountain crushing blow.
Nine steps
Takes Jorð's protector
Before sinking,
By the serpent slain.

One handed
Wolf binder,
Gored by Hel's guardian,
Falls.

The gods' watchman
Wrangling with
The Lie-Smith,
Laufey's son,

Falls and fells
The monster father,
Dying in
Each other's arms.

The sea swallows
The middle garden,
The sky burns black.

While in the woods
Of Hoddmimis Holt
Life and hope
Spring anew.

VI.
It ends
With waves retreating,
The green breaking
Through the blue.
Among Yggdrasil's roots,
At Mimir's well,
New shoots
Will blossom
And grow.

I see
The young gods
Assembling
At the ruins
Of Iðavollr.
The silent wolf slayer,
Alfoðr avenger,
Courageous and mighty
Grandsons of Jorð,
Mjolnir carried between them.
Joined by two
Walking out of Hel
Just to see
The sun shine again.

They speak of
Many things:
Plans for golden thrones,
Majestic halls,
And the secrets
Of Oðinn's runes.

Little left around them,
Charred in the ash,
Save tarnished
Golden checkers
With which
The wise one
Played his game.

Níu Heimar

Níu Heimar, Nine homes,
Nine Worlds the Universe is made.
Through the center Yggdrasil,
The cosmic backbone grows.

At first there was only
Muspelheim, Niflheim
And the gap in between

Muspelheim, home of world wrecker
Surtr and his Eldjötnar,
Fire giants living in volcanic furnaces
Waiting to break Bifröst to bits.

Icy Niflheim, mist-home,
World of dim darkness and fog
Surrounding Hvergelmir,
Bountiful bubbling spring
—filled by dew drops from the rack
of EikÞyrnir, Valhallan stag—
Where lives Níðhǫggr malice-striker;
From where Elivágar flows,
Feeding the rivers of the worlds.

In between in the yawning empty void,
The gaping abyss of Ginnungagap,
Where fire and ice meet
Under the second root of the World Ash,
Arose Ymir Jötnar-föðr,
Aurglemir Æsir enemy,
Murdered by Bor's sons,
Who built the world from his carcass.

Alföðr created Ásgarðr Ásheim,
Æsir-garden god-home,
Foliage planted from seeds found
In Aurglmir's left testicle.

Behind the walls of Ásgarðr
Was Oðinn's shining home.
Glaðsheimr, where stood Valhalla,
Great hall of the slain
Judged by a Valkyrie to be
Worthy of Wotan's army,
Awaiting Ragnarök, meade in hand.

The rest of the battle-fallen
Fly to Freyja's field Fólkvangr.
The other dead approach Ásgarðr not,
Descending instead to Niflhel,
Misty home of Hel Loki-daughter,
In the dark outskirts of Niflheim.

Burning Bifröst shining Ásbrú,
Bridge of gods,
Stretching from Himinbjörg
Heimdallr-home to Midgarðr,
Fortified garden given to the saplings
Of Ask and Embla by High
Just-As-High and Third.
Its walls built of Ymir eyebrows,
Battlements crafted from the nails of his toes
To guard against his progeny living yonder
In Jötunheimr near the sea shore.

Vanaheimr, home of gods,
Álfar-cousins, fertile, wise and far seeing,
Making war with Æsir, Jötnar-born.
Treaties make peace, make friends, make families.
All become one in Ásgarðr, til twighlight falls.

Álfheimr, Elf-home,
Fair, beautiful, glowing and wize,
Its dwellers stand apart and above us all,
Casting a shadow as black as they are light.

North near the mists of Niflheim
On Niðavellir Myrkheim,
The ebony fields where darkness dwells,
In the mines of Svartalfheimr
Are the master craftsmen: The Dvergar
Dwarves, crawling in the earth like
Maggots in the muscle of a frost giant.

Yggdrasil

Heart of the Nine Worlds,
Rooted in the depth of the Earth,
Tended by the Weavers:
Was, Is and Will-be,
Twined together in Destiny,
Watered from the weird well of Fate.
Her branches brushing Bifröst Bridge,
Tickling Heimdall's feet on the front porch of the Æsir.

Wodanaz

I Wodanaz, Wotan, Óðinn Alföðr,
One-eyed Wanderer,
Rune-maker, Warrior-Poet,
Son of Borr Búri-son and
Bestla Bölþorn-daughter,
Who plucked out my left eye for wisdom,
Hung from Yggdrasil for nine nights,
Sacrificing myself to myself, for enlightenment.
With my brothers, Vili and Ve,
Slaughtered Ymir Jötnar-father,
Slitting his throat, draining his blood
Into lakes, rivers, and oceans.
Squeezing out his sweat to season saltwater seas,
Flaying the flesh from his bones to fashion the earth,
Bones boiled bare made into mountains,
Molars and teeth into boulders and rocks,
Trees and forests created from hairs and whiskers.
Crafted Midgard, shelter-fortress for children of Ask and Embla,
From his eyebrows, its gates from his eyelashes,
Battlements from his toenails.
His empty skull we set over the earth
On the shoulders of four dwarves,
Norðri, Suðri, Austri and Vestri,
Forming the vault of the heavens,
Scooping out his brains to make the clouds in the sky.

High, Just As High; Third (Tanka)

Odin, Vili; Ve
Wōðanaz, Wiljô, Wīhą
Slayed and flayed Ymir
Crafted Asgard and Midgard
Breathed life into Ash and Elm.

Huginn and Muninn (Haiku)

Two ravens fly out
Watching all under the sky
And returning home.

The Promise of the Runes

Looking at reflections in jagged shards
Of a shattered mirror,
The fall of twilight's shadow
Grows ever nearer,
But when you see the reaping angel
There's no real reason to fear her.
Remember the words and visions
Of the blind Nordic seer,
The promises made of runes
Sworn on the life of Sleipnir:

Bridges will burn, stars will fall,
Witness it with your own eyes.
Life wanes, blood flows,
Darkness alone fills the skies.
Smoke will settle, the fires cool,
And the Sun will once again rise.

Mother Frigg

Oh dear Frigg, Oðinn wife,
Bold Baldr and blind Höðr mother,
Are you wise Wodan's first wife
Or his second?
You're a mother and you're of the Earth,
Are you Móðir Jorð, thunder mother?
Are are you lady Freyja, Óðr wife,
Njörðr daughter, Freyr sister,
Mother of treasured daughters,
Hnoss and Gersemi,
Keeper of Fólkvangr field,
Where dwell the half of the honored dead
That don't belong to Oðinn?

Beloved Æsir Queen, Vanir princess,
Did Wōđanaz wed you to seal the peace?
Did he love you as an
Alföðr loves his Jorð Móðir?
Did his eye see you for who you are?

Þórr

Born of a meeting between Earth and Sky,
Mother Jörð and Alföðr Óðinn,
Thunderer Þórr, Jötun Slayer,
Lightening Wielder, Relentless red-headed warrior.

Wheat-haired Sif husband,
One-eyed Wotan son,
Valkrie Þrúðr father,
Beloved Baldr brother.

With Mjölnir mountain-crusher,
Dvergr forged lightening-hammer,
Iron glove wielded stubby handled serpent slayer.

Stand at the end of the world,
Stopping Midgard strangling sea serpent,
Jörmungandr Ragnarök-starter
Hel-brother, Loki-son,
With your next to last breath.

Not a goldilocks Hemsworth
Shakespeare-speaking superhero.
But a fire-haired, goat-cart riding,
Mankind protecting, Troll smashing
Champion of Asgard:
þunraz Thunderer.

Mjölnir (Haiku)

Mighty Mjölnir
Thunderer Þorr's war hammer
Jörmungandr's bane

Loki, Oðinn Brother

Loki Loptr Lóðurr,
Roaring Hveðrungr,
Trickster lord of air and fire.
Sky walking lie smith
Laufey-son, Jötunn spawn,
Fenrir father, Sleipner mother
Serpent sire, Hel father.
Blood brother to the Alföðr.
Jötnar by birth, Æsir by choice.

Tricks and games, schemes and jokes
That end in death and pain.
Golden wigs and short handled hammers,
Þorr dressed in Freyja's wedding dress,
Frigg's tears at Baldr's grave.

Loki bound his son's intestines,
Sigyn catching the venom
Dripping from the fangs of the snake
Skaði hung over his head,
every hundredth drop burning his forehead,
While his wife empties her bowl,
Writhing in pain, shaking the ground,
Waiting for the Universe to end.

Tyr

Tīwaz, Tīw, Tyr
One handed war god,
Guardian of Justice and Law,
Gave the Wolf his right hand
As compensation for damages
When he was by the gods with Gleipnir bound.

Tīwaz Föðr, Dyeus Phater
Sky-father reigning
Before the Alföðr
As Tuesday precedes Wednesday,
A shining sky given over to
The one-eyed warrior poet
And the working-class thunderclap.

Tīwaz, Tvaṣṭṛ, Tuisto
Born of the earth,
Builder of the heavens,
Father of man,
Grandfather of kings.

When twilight falls,
Gleipnir breaks,
And Wodan is swallowed whole,
The Wolf-Children
Will murder the sun and moon,
While the one-handed warrior
Is laid low by Garmr,
The hound of Hel.

Óðrœrir (a Tanka)

Kvasir, the wisest
Born of Æsir and Vanir
Slain by jealous dwarves
Blood brewed into honey-wine:
Óðinn's mead of poetry.

Staring into the Flames.

Raging fires of Muspelheim
Flaming sword of Surtr,
Gentle beautiful glow
Of destruction peering over the ridge.

A brigade of brave warriors,
Oath sworn to **Móðir** Jorð,
Stand ready in defense
Of her ancient holy lodge,
Prepared to give no quarter
And surrender no ground,
Facing down the Eldjötnar,
The sons of Muspel,
Tearing through the forests of Freyja,
Burning Miðgarð black.

Oðinn's army,
Children of Ash and Elm,
Siblings of Oak and Fir,
Stand at the edge of Ragnarok
Without fear.

Winter Solstice Wild Hunt

Langbarðr Óðinn jólfaðr,
Long-bearded Odin Yule-father,
Leading the winter solstice Wild Hunt,
One-eyed Wodan's Wild Gift Giving Ride,
Riding Sleipnir alongside stallions, goat-carts,
And sleighs pulled by reindeer,
With Grecian Niklaus wonder-worker,
Children's saint, Christmas-father,
Shoulder to shoulder with Dutch-brother
Sinterklaas, his twin Kris Kringle Christkind,
And Amerikanisch Santa Clause.

Celebrating a savior's birth,
The Horned God's rebirth,
Or just happy the Sun wasn't swallowed by a wolf,
Ghostly riders in the sky
Traveling across the inside of Ymir's skull.

Near the end of the parade,
Beyond the gift-givers and ghosts,
Behind the gray rider with the elvish staff,
Comes the justice-bringers,
Led by Krampus Hel-son,
Goat-horned grandson of Loki,
Faithful Æsir-servant, law-protector,
Bells on his cloak ring a warning
As he beats misbehaving children
With birch branches and bundling
The truly wicked into wicker baskets,
Or into friend Zwarte Piet's sack,
To be taken to his mother's realm,
Be drowned or be dinner for the hoard.

Frau Perchta, snow white maiden or
Hideous shriveled crone,
Krampus' alpine queen,
Handing out shiny silver coins
To all who've been good;
Disemboweling and stuffing guts with straw
To all who have not.

He knows when you're sleeping,
He sees all you do when you're awake,
He'll know if you've been bad or not,
So be good, if just for your own sake.

Burrowers in the Deep

Svartálfar,
Álfar who prefer
Blackness of night
To the light of day.
Cave living,
Mine working,
Excavating precious gems and minerals
For their smiths.
Hammers, spears,
And enchanted golden wigs
Exported to Asgard?

Dvergar,
Born of the blood of Brimir
And the bones of Bláinn,
maggots burrowing
In the flesh of Ymir's corpse?

Dwarrows,
Dwellers of the dark fields of Niðavellir,
Mystic Myrkheim, darkness home,
In the comfort of the caves of Svartálfheim?

Short, stocky, ill-tempered craftsmen,
Working the mines of Moria
In ancient Khazad-dûm?

Diminutive Disney dwarfs,
Thatch roof cottage in the Enchanted Forrest
Whistling their way to work?

Or massive men bearing the weight
Of the vault of the sky,
Scooped out jötunn skull,
On broad shoulders
Standing on the four corners
Of the compass rose?

Ragnarök

Three cocks crow, echoing from
Asgard, Jötunheimr, and Hel.
Yggdrasil shudders its ashen roots,
The world worm writhes in anticipation
Drowning the shores of mankind.

Shadows fall over Midgard,
The sun shines black.
Men's blood stains brothers' swords,
Skulls cleaved by uncles' axes,
No mercy shown, none received.
Death is all we know.

Heimdall's horn sounds the alarm
From the guardhouse on Bifrost Bridge.
One-eyed warrior Woden calls his war council,
Consulting wise Mimir's head.
Ready for the battle he's prepared for
His entire life.

Naglfar, the ship built from the toenails and fingernails
Of ten thousand dead men, sets sail the seas of fate,
Chaos as cargo, Loki stands at the wheel.
Surt and kin march out of Muspelheim single-file
To hide their numbers.

Æsir murmur amongst themselves,
Dwarves stand in stone doorways groaning,
Alfar are nowhere to be seen.

Fenrir breaks his chains and
Swallows the Alföðr whole,
Þórr slays the mighty Midgard worm
Nine feet from his own death.

Blood soaked sun sets in the west,
Stars fall from the sky,
Ocean overtakes dry land,
As history comes to an end.

But, the Seeress sings,
Midgard will rise above the waves,
Brave Baldar will breathe again,
As the sun shines on the golden game pieces
That the gods played with in bygone days.

Wars in Heaven

I. Uranus and Kronos

Worsanos, Ouranos,
Uranus, divine rain maker
Standing on high.
Heavens born of Aether and Earth,
--or perhaps just Earth—
Generated from chaotic chasms
In the Night.

Brother of the sea,
Father of the ocean stream.
Son of his consort,
Bedding her on the horizon.

Where Heaven and Earth meet,
Were born giants, monsters, and gods:

Twelve mighty Titans,
In their father's image born,
His commands they would surely obey.

Three circle-eyed Kyklopes,
Bright, Thunder, and Lightening.
Skilled smiths forging
Thunderbolts, sunlight and moonbeams.

And three fifty-headed
Hundred-handed monstrosities,
So terrible to behold
That Father Sky
Pushed them back
Into Mother Earth's womb.

Mother Gaia,
In anguish and in pain,
Asked the youngest
Of her eldest children,
Crafty Kronos,
To see justice done.

With an adamantine sickle,
Fashioned by his mother,
Kronos castrated the Sky
Tossing the testicles away
To be swallowed up
By his uncle, the Sea.

Drops of blood
From the open wound
Became Erinyes, Furies, Eumenides,
Kindly spirits of vengeance and death.
While semen foamed up
From Pontos' throat,
Birthing Aphrodite,
Goddess of love.

Kronos, now the king,
Kept his ugly brethren
Imprisoned
In his mother's womb.

Gaia wailed
As eunuched *Uranus squeaked,*
"I hope you have a son
Who's just like you!"

II. Kronos and Zeus

Six babies Rhea bore,
Five siblings crook'd Kronos swallowed,
Devoured for fear of being deposed
As his father was,
As the Fates decreed
He would be.

But the sixth sibling was,
By grandmother Gaia, saved.
Born in secret on Crete.
In a cave beneath Mt. Ida
By tender Almaltheia raised.
While regal Rhea presented Kronos
With a swaddled stone to swallow.

And in the secret places
Deep within the earth,
The young prince waited
And trained
And learned
And grew
Strong, steady, and wise.

And at the appointed time,
When he could weild the sickle-sword
That castrated the sky,
And bear the great shield, Aegis,
Made from the stretched leather
Of Almaltheia's goat,
With instruction from
Metis, mother of Wisdom.
Into the palace atop Mt Othrys
He would sneak

As the King's cupbearer disguised,
And into Kronos' chalice
Pour Metis' mixture
Of spicy mustard,
Sweet wine,
And secrets,
Dislodging first,
Rhea's stone,
Which landed near Mt. Parnassus
In Delphi, where Pythia
To Apollo would one day prophesy,
And then her five children,
Now fully grown
And eager to join
Their brave brother's quest
For justice and revenge.

Down in the darkest
Depths of Tartarus
They would set free
Their lost uncles,
One-eyed and Hundred-Handed,
Long ago unjustly imprisoned
By their father
And grandfather.

Grateful circle-eyed Arges
Gifted the prince
With thunderbolts and lightning
With which to wage war
On their jailors.

For ten years
The thunder would roll
Until the Titans were banished
To Tartarus,
To be guarded
By their hundred-handed brothers.

A new golden throne
Over Olympus now stood,
Where sat the prince,
Now reigning as king,
Forever suspicious
Of any offspring
Who seemed cleverer
Than he.

Shadow and Light

An old darkness
Weaves her webs,
Strands and cables
From rock to tree
Covering the valley
From cliff to cliff,
A blackness no light can penetrate,
No eye can pierce.

Under cover of clouds
Of shadow, darkness, and void,
Led by her Master, full of
Ego, greed, and revenge.

Piercing, sucking dry
The light of the world,
Licking up the bleeding sap
From the trees of life.

The only light left,
Stolen away; hidden.
A world draped in darkness; marred.
Waiting to be healed.

Of Alfar and Dvergar

Alβiz Alfar Föðr,
Born of moonbeams
Dancing on the fog of the forest
Near the river of Rhun,
Patriarch to seven brothers and sisters
Awoken on the riverbank.

Married Đanuz, earth mother,
Daughter of sunlight
Refracted off the dew drops
Dripping from a rose petal.

Five sons, two daughters
And six cities founded,
One in the northwest of the world,
Where the ravens would one day flock,
One near Þurisaz's realm,
Where the High King would one day reign,
And four in the north of the world,
Where the Alfar would flee
After chaos, fire and death
Drove them from the valley
Of their birth.

Falʒaz the wise, student of Nature,
Keeper of her secrets.
Defender of the sacred
Stone of fate,
Wielder of the Sword of Light,
Forged for his father
By Durinn of Twerias,
Son of his brother Đwerʒaz,

So the king could
Cut through the night.

Warrior twins, Gorʒaz and Finɖʒaz,
Defending their tribes
With the Spear of Fire
And Lance of Thunder,
Against which
No army can stand.

Murʒaz the healer;
Cultivator of fruits,
vegetables, and lamb.
Cradling the cauldron,
Hallowed hamper
Of Gwyddno Garahir,
The great bowl of Bivurr,
From which no one ever
Walks away hungry.

βanʒuz, mother of the royal line,
Where runes are written,
Before Wodan was hung,
Where the Earth will rise
And with Æsir blood mix,
As the thunder crushes the sky.

Alβʒuz, white queen
Of the west
Named for her father,
Founder of the kingdom
Where his glory
Will blossom and grow.

Đwerȝaz Dvergar Föðr,
Molding metals as if so much clay.
Dug out the labyrinth
Underground mine-city
Of Twerias,
Under the misty plains of Niðavellir,
Where Móðsognir dug,
Searching for metals and gems
For Durinn to forge and mold
Into Swords and spears,
Cups and cauldrens,
War hammers and wigs,
For elves, men, and gods.
Treasures kept in city vaults
Until their time of need.

Four treasures for Alfheim,
Destined for Éire.
Thirteen treasures for Albion
And the children of Prydein..
Six treasures for Asgard,
Forged in mischief,
Powerless to save them from their doom.

Mother Danu

Danuvios, Danu
Donwy; Don.

Wife of
Albigos, Belgios,
Beli; Bile.

Daughter of
Abnoba
And Mathonwy the wise.

Sister of
Renos, Rhon, and Math.

Life giver,
Thirst quencher,
Nurturer of
Murias' fields.

Matron of
The four jewels
Of the north.

Fay Queen
Of Beli's honeyed isle,
Whose fair family,
The Tylwyth Teg,
Arrived from the sea
Sailing ships
Made of mist and fire,
Ruling these lands

Until the coming of man
Drove them underground,
Forcing them to retreat
To the apple covered isles
Of the west.

Blessed Bran

Bran, blessed crow,
Revered raven,
Son of the seas,
Brother of Branwen,
Defender of honor,
Keeper of the cauldron
Of life.

Gave your sister's hand
In marriage to Eriu's land,
Revoked once the abuse
Of the King was clear.

After the battle
That broke your sister's heart,
Your disembodied head,
Cleaved from his neck
By a friend,
Talking and joking,
Keeping his comrades company
On the long
Journey home.

After 87 years
The sorrow settles in.
A silent head
Laid to rest
Under the White Hill,
Gazing toward Gaul,
Protecting and defending
Even in death.

The Raven, the Eagle, and the Red Dragon

The legions of the Eagle
Will come
To the bless'd Raven's home,
Shackling the land
And its people,
Burning their sacred groves.

The Eagle lives in an aerie
Of gleaming gold,
Yet covets humble cottages
With a thirst for power
And glory,
For no sake
But its own.

The Raven and its flock
Will resist and fight
Alongside a pride of lions
From the high white land
To the north.

Confronting the Eagle
On fields of battle,
And from behind
Rocks and trees,
Taken back
To the Eagle's loft
In iron chains,
Or disappearing
Into the woods
To fight another day.

The Eagle will place
The Lion's pride
Behind a guarded wall,
Fearing he might
Get bitten
Or crushed
By a mighty paw.

The Raven will be
Smothered and subdued
Under the yoke
Of the Eagle's love,
Until the day
The great golden aerie
Collapses
Under its own
Bloated weight.
Abandoning the Raven
To its own devices
And a host of enemies
Born anew.

The Raven will transform
Becoming a fiery
Dragon of red.
Facing the White Wyrm
Of Woden's brood,
He himself invited
Into his home.

A bear
Born of a boar
Will raise
The Red Dragon's banner,

Pushing the Wyrm
Back to the beaches,
Seemingly beaten,
Though the moment
Will be brief.

The back of the Dragon
Will be broken,
Its people will be pushed
To the edge of the world.

The people of the Dragon
Will wait and pray
For the Bear to return,
And deliver them
From their fate,
To return them
To the Raven's rule.

The Dragons of Dinas Emrys

Gwrtheyrn, Vortigern,
Traitor king of Britain,
Fleeing savage Saxon soldiers,
Mercinaries he hired to harrass
Scots and Pictish pirates
To the ruin of us all.

Flee to Gwynedd, scoundrel king
To Dinas Ffaraon, Unfortunate usurper
Build a fortress to protect you
From your sins.
But the towers won't stand,
The foundation will not hold,
Battlements built in the day,
Lay in rubble by the morn.

Your wise men,
such as they are,
Suggest slaughtering
A fatherless child,
Blood soaked foundation stones,
They say,
Will stand strong
Against Saxon spears.

So search the land they do
For your selfish salvation
Until, in the field of Aelecti,
Between the Usk and the Rumney,
Emrys is found.

A boy who
Rumor tells
Has no father,
Though he himself says
The Roman purple
His parents wore,

Proving the king's men
As wise
As thier liege is brave.

So back to Snowdonia
Emrys is taken,
His fate to meet.

But die
The boy did not,
Regardless of paternity.
Gifted through awen
He was
With visions of prophecy.

He saw true
The cause
Of this sad King's grief.

"Under the hill
On which this fort
Is built,
Two vases in a pool
Together stuck,
Within the vases
A tent;

Within the tent
Two dragons of old,
Placed there for safety
By old King Lludd,
In times before
The Eagle landed.

For the warmth
Of the tent
The two dragons fight.
The battle disturbing
The ground above,
Weakening the foundation,
Toppling the walls.

The red dragon is Briton
And ours,
The white dragon is Saxon
And thiers.
The tent is your kingdom,
Fight for it they do,
Fight for it you must,
But not here
And not now.
This land is mine."

Merlin

Merlin, oh Merlin,
Where did you go?
Do you seek the wisdom of the Raven
And the courage of the Crow?

Did fay Nimue entrap you
In that ancient crystal cave?
Do you dream 'neath the hills of Prydein
Of all the lives you failed to save?

Or did Vivian imprison you
In a tall tower or oaken tree,
To spend eternity pondering
All the fates you failed to see?

But could even you have stopped
The slaughter on the fields of Camlann,
The blood drawn, the kingdom lost,
On that wicked day destiny damned?

You put Arthur on the throne,
Twas history that threw him down,
Leaving only pale pretenders
To try and grasp Prydein's crown.

A Song of Taliesin

I was a grain of wheat
In Cerridwen's belly
That grew into a man.
Gwion Bach devoured,
Reborn with a radiant brow.

She sought to inspire
And I was inspired.
Inspiration meant for another,
But fate had other plans.

I stirred her Cauldron of Awen,
Its contents burned
Opening eyes and mind.

I was there
When the universe
Was a white-hot grain,
And will be there
When it is an ice-cold cloud
Spread thin by time.

I was there
In the valley of Rhun,
Before the years had been numbered,
By the shores of sunlight
When the fair ones
First gazed upon the trees.

I saw the sword of light
Forged by the sons of Twerios.
I saw the son of Vandar
Buried in the earth.
Family fragmented
Along the shores dispersed

I was there
When the flood waters came
And Cessair by Bandba was saved.
While Elfhame vanished
Under the waves.

I saw sister Alba
Lost in a foreign land.
Rescued by a knight
From the end of the world,
Reunited with her mother
She would be.

I was there
When Bran crossed the sea
To restore his sister's honor.
I heard steel strike steel,
I saw the blood river run.

I sailed home
With Manawydan and Pryderi
To bury the king's head
Facing the foreign lands.

I was there
When Degfed and Lleu
Sailed to Elfhame's remnants

To make uncle Nudd whole.
The Sword of Light
Weilded by a silver hand,
Brother against brother,
To restore their uncle to the throne.

I saw the black blades forged
By twerger hands alone,
For Caswallawn
And the wealthy wolf
To drive the dark ones
From their home.

I saw a king
Seduced by chaos,
Abandoning justice;
Giving rise to a Dark Queen,
Dressed in green,
Bathing a kingdom
In self-indulgence,
Decadence and greed.

I was there
When Albrennin
Threw down his cousin
By the black blade of Blaidd,
Watching his sea fortress burn,
A fire he lit
From a far younger land.

I watched
As he walked away
Into wilderness,
Into legends and dreams.

I witnessed his seed,
Clothed in white,
Bathed in light,
Wisdom at her side,
Rise from the Reinos
To reclaim the land,
Replanting the sacred oak.

I was there
When the sons of Nemed landed
At the mouth of the Ituna.
Welcomed by fair Queen Uonaidh,
As if she'd been expecting them
All this time.
Giving them her kingdom
And her daughters,
As Prydein gave his name
To the land.

I was there
When Lludd and Lleflys
Found the dragons
Whose screams filled the land.
I saw them bound and buried
So that, by Emrys,
they later could be found.

I saw the Raven's brood
Fighting amongst themselves,
Clawing for control.
I was there when they delivered
Prydein's precinct
Into the talons of the Eagle,

To be wrapped in chains
For its own protection.

I was there
On the Shady Isle
Watching the sacred oak groves burn.
I felt the druidic tears
Fall into the fires.

I was there
When the Eagle fell,
Diseased from within,
Devoured from without.
Abandoning us
To our own devices.

I saw the traitor king
Try to tame the White Dragon
To fight off the pirates
Of Alba and Éire,
Wedding its spawn,
To the damnation of us all.

I saw the coward king
Fleeing to the west
With his wisemen,
To the castle whose walls
Would not hold.

I was there,
I saw the fear in his eyes,
When young Emrys
Foretold his fate.

I was there
At Badon
When Arthur earned his name.
I heard the cheers,
I smelled the blood,
And I knew it wouldn't last.

I was there
On the Prydwen with Arthur,
Sailing to Eire or Annwn,
To rescue, to pillage,
And to have glory got.

I was there
At Camlann,
I saw Arthur fall.
Misunderstandings and murder,
Disintegration of the land.

I was there
When Gwion Bach
Stirred the Cauldron of Cerridwen
For an entire year.

I saw him burn,
I saw him alight.
I saw him devoured,
I saw him reborn.

I was there
When Elphin found the babe
And raised him as his own.
I heard him give the boy a name:
Taliesin.

Excerpt from the Tale of Myrddin Wyllt

I. The Aftermath of Arfderydd

I, the son of Madog Morfryn,
Went mad on the fields of Arfderydd,
Where Gwenddoleu fell.

Cursed by God some say am I,
For what on that battlefield befell
My king, my friends, and family dear
Overwhelming me with despair.

Touched by madness they say I am
For the part I played in it all.
My penance for planning a battle
Which broke shoulders and bled hearts.

But cause this catastrophe, I did not,
Though many regrets I have
In service to my sire, my duty I did
On the field of battle we found ourselves on.

Not there were we to fight Saesons,
From the lands we lost,
Nor Scots nor Picts
Raiding from the sea.

There we faced Cymry,
Our countrymen,
Whose fathers fought together
Under the Dragon Banner
With Emrys and Arthur
At Badon Hill
Where Ælle did fall.

Remembered our reasons won't be,
All but forgot, our cherished cause,
Our legacy, a futile fighting
Second only to the disaster of Camlann.

Blood and broken bodies I saw
When Gwyn's ravens did scream,
Mourning my mother's children,
As a shroud on my sister's son I place.

Gwenddoleu and Gwendydd
Will love me no more,
Rhydderch will demand my head.

The young girl I gathered apples with
Is far beyond my reach,
Never shine the sun will again,
The darkness falls at my feet.

A voice was whispering low
On a fay wind-blown.
Not sure was I from where it came,
A god, a soldier, an angel of the Lord,
Or even if it was my own.

Of the true cause it spoke
Of the shadow that fell,
But face it I could not.
Run I did to Celyddon's woods
Away from any face that could speak.
Through the trees, among the beasts,
There to live out my days.

II. Myrddin's Song

By madness and grief taken was I
Into the heart of the darkest wood.
Apart, alone, but abandoned not,
I scavenged like a common crow.

Sipping from a stream, to slake a thirst,
That from Ceridwen's well did spring,
Blessed was I by Awen's hand
With visions no one else could see.
To know all things is to lose one's mind
If not lost it already was.

I saw the seed Ceridwen swallowed,
I saw Gwion grow in her womb.
I saw the shining brow rescued by Elphin,
I saw and understood.

I was the moon-light reflection
On the river of Don.
I was a stone, into the water thrown,
I was the waves on the pond.

I was the sharp of the sword,
I was the straight of the spear.
I was the sound of her laughter,
I was the salt of her tears.

I was a daisy in the pasture
Looking toward the sun.
I was a hare moving faster
Than a greyhound on the run.

I was the son of the sea-crow
Bran gave his head to save.
I was the walls of the sea-fort
Vortigern gave away.

I was Sophia's salmon
Demne fried for Fintan.
I was the grain of wheat
That grew into a man.

III. Myrddin's Lament

Tirelessly hunted me Rhydderch's men did
Through all the acres of Celyddon's woods,
But seen I'm not unless desire I do,
So, in Afallach's arms I safely sit.

Well-trodden are these trails
Many footsteps here have fallen,
Searchers, Seekers, hunters, and prey.
Questing a grail, a beast,
Or a safe passage home,
Finding only what they take with them.

The soldiers seek Rhydderch's revenge
For the beloved son who fell in battle,
The sister-son I recognized not
Until it was far too late.

Gwendydd's tears burn my cheeks;
Rhydderch's rage consumes me.
Never again to look into thine eyes
And see not the pain I placed there.

The ravens of Gwyn shadow my steps,
The howl of his hounds I hear.
The fallen he escorts to Annwfn's shores,
But left alone with my madness am I.

Where soldiers were slain, I have stood,
From Camlann to Arfderydd.
Arthur lies in Avalon
Under Morgan's healing hands.
Gwenddoleu lies in his grave
Under a cold Carnedd of stones.

I hide, a hunted man,
Among the apple trees.

For great oak groves I searched,
To divine the truth as in days of old.
Why was I left behind
By the raven hoard of Annwfn?
Why am I alone not allowed to die?

But those mighty oak groves,
And those who their secrets held,
Are nowhere now to be found
Outside the fay shores of Afallach's isle.
Burnt they were long ago
By the legions of the she-wolf's son,
An age before the Eagle rotted from within.

IV. Gwendydd's Song

Visions he sees so clearly
From Awen's ancient throne
By the carpenter's son sent.
Of answers to questions unasked,
Of things unknown, unseen,
And yet to be.
Of the stars and their courses,
Of the circles of the world
And what lies beyond.

But of the here and now
And a woman's heart
He's as blind as old man Morda
Stoking the fire beneath Ceridwen's cauldron
While its contents by Gwion are stirred.

Alone he believes himself to be,
Hunted by my husband,
Hated by his sister,
Forgotten by his beloved,
Abandoned to madness
Among the apple trees.

My dear lonely Llallwgan,
So much lately have we lost:
Brothers, son, and comrades close.
Long shall we carry the scars.

So little family have I left:
A husband, a daughter,
And one last brother
Lost among birds and beasts.

My king blames not the bard
For the battle that bore his heir away.
My king blames not the bard
Who faithfully followed his lord
Onto the field that day.

And I blame not my brother
Who, blinded by the battle,
Recognized not his own blood
Until it stained his scarlet blade.

So, I send out the king's soldiers
To search for my lost Llallwgan
In the frozen forest of Celyddon
And sing to him
His sister's song.

Under the Sídhe

Outside the cities
Under the cairn covered
Hollow hills of Eire,
The Aes Sídhe sit
In mansions bigger
Than the hills
They're built under.

Driven underground
By distant cousins,
Who took the island by force,
Naming it for the ancient enemy
They worshipped
Among sacred oaks

Driven underground,
But not the dark damp
Underground of worms, bugs,
And corpses.
Nor the dark black
Caverns of Twerg miners.

Rather, underground,
Under the sidhe,
To the very deep
Of the Otherworld of Annwn
Where time stands still
And youth never fades.

Driven across the
Western sea,
Through Manannan's fog,
Past the ninth wave
To Tir na nOg,
Where Myrddin
Took twelve treasures
And Oisin took
Four jewels,
To the glass palace
Near the sacred apple groves
Where gods and kings sleep
Waiting to return.

Driven away
By the followers of
A jealous foreign god,
Who'd brook no rivals.
An enemy more
Cunning and subtle
Than any Formorian.
An incursion not recorded
In the *Book of Invasions,*
Which was redacted
By the victors.

Driven and diminished
In substance and size,
Demoted
From Gods
To kings,
From physical
Forces of nature
To ephemeral,
Transparent
Fairies and sprites,
Fallen angels
Cast out of the light.
Lucky little leprechauns
Hording pots of gold
At the rainbow's end,
Or a rainbow of marshmallows
And sugar filled
Cereal bowls
For your breakfast table.

Outside,
Under the hollow hills of Eire.
The Aes Sídhe sit
And wait.

Twilight Visions

A one-armed Odin-eyed
Mad martyr prophet,
Blinded for wisdom,
Crippled for sin.
Stands at the edge of the abyss,
Witnessing, with the one eye
He no longer has,
The Wyrd White Wyrm
Strangle creation;
Digesting time.

At twilight
The ravens, crows, and rooks
Gather and wait
While the stars fall,
Blue diamonds
Plunging through
The black velvet sky.

Grandsons rise up
Against grandfathers,
Slitting their throats
Before their fathers
Are conceived.

Chaos and Paradox burn
The charred corpse of causality,
Cause following effect,
Yesterday arrives tomorrow,
Tomorrow just a memory;
Today is nothing at all.

All the moments
From death 'til birth
Collapsing into themselves,
Folding into a singularity:
The final moment.

On the field of truth,
Among the ruins of life,
Darkness rises
And silence falls,
The Question remains
Unanswered.

Appendix I: Pronunciation Guide

Name	Pronunciation	Notes
Abnoba	Av-nova	Gaulish. River Goddess. Mother of Danuvios.
Æliz	Ale-iz	Brother of Alßiz
Aes Sídhe	Ees Shee	Irish Gaelic. The People of the Sídhe (i.e. The Tuatha de Dannan
Æsir	Aye-seer	Norse. The Gods
Aether	Ay-ther ("th" as in Thor)	Greek Αἰθήρ "Upper Sky" Primordial God of Air. Possible father of Uranus.
Afallach	Av-ahl-ock	Welsh. "The Apple One" King of Ynys Afallach, the Isle of Apples, which is also known as the Isle of Avalon
Albigos	Al-bee-gose	Indo-European. Husband of Danuvios
Albrennin	Al-bren-in	Gaulish. "Elf-King" Related to the Old High German Alberich, from which the

		name Oberon is ultimately derived.
Alfar	Alf-are	Norse. Elves.
Álfarfoðr	Alf-ar-foth-er ("th" as in this)	Norse. "Father of Elves" Title of Alβiz
Alfgarð	Alf-garth ("th" as in this)	Norse. "Elf Garden" First city of the Alfar (Elves)
Álfheimr	Alf-Haym	Norse. "Elf Home"
Álfheimr	Alf-haym	Norse. "Elf Home" Realm of the Alfar (Elves)
Alföðr	All-foth-er ("th" as in this)	Norse. "All Father" Title of Odin.
Almaltheia	Al-mal-they-ya	Greek Ἀμάλθεια "Tender Goddess" Foster Mother of Zeus.
Alβiz	Al-vhiz	Father of the Alfar.
Alβ3uz	Alv-yuz	Daughter of Alβiz. Sometimes called Alvias, Albia, or Alba.
Angrboða	Ang-both-ah ("th" as in this)	Norse. "She who offers sorrow" Jotun. Mother of Fenrir, Hel, and Jormungandr by Loki.

Annwfn	Ah-noo-vin	Welsh. "The Not World" The Otherworld; land of the Dead. Ruled by Gwyn ap Nudd.
Annwn	Ah-noon	Welsh. Alternate spelling of Annwfn.
Anþaraz	An-thar-az ("th" as in Thor)	"The Other One" Brother of Alßiz.
Aphrodite	Af-row-dye-tea	Greek. Ἀφροδίτη (Possibly of Semitic origin). Goddess of Love.
Apollo	Uh-paul-oh	Greek Ἀπόλλων Son of Zeus. Brother of Artemis. God of poetry, prophecy, music, dance, et. Al.
Arfderydd	Arv-der-ith ("th" as in this)	Welsh. Site of a disastrous battle amongst the Brythonic Welsh kings in 573.
Arges	Ar-geez	Greek. Ἄργης "Bright" Son of Uranus and Gaia. One of the three Kyklopes.
Ásbrú	As-bru	Norse. "Bridge of the Gods" Another name for the Bifrost.

Ásgarðr	As-garth ("th" as in this)	Norse. "Garden of the Æsir" Asgard.
Ásheimr	As-haym	Norse. "God Home" Asgard
Ask and Embla	Ask & Embla	Norse. "Ash and Elm" The first humans, who were carved from trees.
Aurgelmir	Our-gel-meer ("g" as in get)	Norse. Alias of Ymir
Austri	Aws-tree	Norse. "East" One of four Dvergar who hold up the sky.
Awen	Ah-when	Welsh. Poetic/Prophetic inspiration; enlightenment.
Baldr	Bald-er	Norse. Son of Odin and Frigg
Banba	Ban-uh-buh	Irish Gaelic. One of three patron Goddesses of Ireland, along with her sisters Ériu and Fódla
Belgios	Bel-ge-os	Gaulish. Early version of the name Beli
Beli	Bell-ee	Welsh. King of Britain. Husband of Dôn.

Bestla	Bes-tla	Norse. Wife of Borr. Mother of Odin, Vili, and Ve
Bifrost	Bye-frost	Norse. "Shimmering Path" The burning rainbow bridge that connects Asgard with Midgard.
Bilé	Bye-lay	Irish Gaelic. Husband of Danu.
Bivurr	Bye-ver	Norse. Dvergr
Blaidd	Blayth ("th" as in this)	Welsh "wolf" Son of Degfed
Bláinn	Bl-ayn	Norse. Possible alias of Ymir
Bölþorn	Ball-thorn	Norse. "Evil Thorn" A Jotun. Father of Bestla. Grandfather of Odin.
Borr	Boar	Norse. Father of Odin. Husband of Bestla.
Brimir	Bry-meer	Norse. Possible alias of Ymir.
Búri	Boo-ree	Norse. "Producer" or "Father" Father of Borr, grandfather of Odin.
Carnedd	Car-neth ("th" as in this)	Welsh. A Cairn.

Caswallawn	Cash-wa-hlon	Welsh. Early King of Britain. Son of Beli. Brother of Nudd.
Celyddon	Kel-uh-thon ("th" as in this).	Welsh. The Caledonian Forrest.
Ceridwen	Ker-id-when	Welsh. "Crooked Woman" or "Blessed Song" Enchantress and brewer of the Cauldron of Awen.
Cessair	Kes-seer	Irish Gaelic. One of the first invaders of Ireland
Cymry	Cum-ri	Welsh. "Fellow-Countrymen"
Danu	Dan-oo	Irish Gaelic. Wife of Bile. Mother Goddess of the Tuatha de Dannan. Cognate with the Welsh Dôn.
Danuvios	Dan-oo-vee-oss	Indo-European. River Goddess. Wife of Albigos
Đanuz	Than-ooze ("th" as in this)	Mother of the Alfar (Elves). See also Danu and Dôn
Degfed	Deg-ved	Welsh "tenth" A prince of Britain.

Delphi	Del-fee	Greek. Δελφοί "Womb" Location of the Temple of Apollo and the Delphian Oracle, Pythia.
Demne		
Dinas Emrys	Dye-ness Em-riss	Welsh "Emrys' Fort" or "Ambrose's Fort"
Dinas Ffaraon	Dye-ness Far-a-on	Welsh. "Pharaoh's Fort" Early name for Dinas Emrys
Dôn	Don	Welsh. Daughter of Mathonwy. Wife of Beli. Mother of, among others, Gwydion, Arianrhod, and Gilfaethwy.
Donwy	Don-oo-ee	Welsh. Wife of Belgios. Possibly another name for Dôn.
Durinn	Dur-Inn	Son of Đwerʒaz. A Dverg (Dwarf) smith.
Dvergar	Dv-erg-ar	Norse. Dwarves.
Dvergr	Dv-erg	Norse. Dwarf.
Dwarrows	Dwar-rows	Hypothetical plural for Dwarf, coined by J.R.R. Tolkien.

Dwarves		Alternate plural for Dwarf, popularized by J.R.R. Tolkien.
Dweorg	Dwey-org	Old English. Dverg
Đwerʒaz	Thwer-yaz ("th" as in this)	Son of Alßiz. Father of the Dvergar (Dwarves).
Dyeus	Day-yoose	Proto-Indo European. "Day-Light Sky" See also: Zeus and Tiwaz
Dyeus Phater	Day-yoose Fa-ter	Proto-Indo European. "Father of the Day-Light Sky" or "Sky Father" Reflected in the Greek Ζεῦ πάτερ (Zeus Pater) and the Italic *Djous-patēr, which became the Latin Iupiter (Jupiter).
EikÞyrnir	Ayk-thear-near	Norse "Oak-Thorny" A great stag who stands atop Valhalla
Éire	Ay-ra	Irish Gaelic. Ireland. Named for the goddess Éiru.

Eldjötnar	Eld-jote-nar	Norse. "Fire Jotnar" The people of Surtr. Commonly called Fire Giants.
Elfhame	Elf-hayme	Middle English "Elf Home" Álfrheim
Elivágar	El-i-vag-ar	Norse. "Ice Waves" The rivers that existed in Ginnungagap at the beginning of time.
Éljúðnir	El-youth-near	Norse. "Sprayed with Snowstorms" Hall of Hel in Nifleheim (or Niflehel, or Niflehelheim)
Elphin	El-fin	Welsh. Adopted father of Taliesin
Emrys	Em-riss	Welsh form of Abrose/Ambrosius. A young Welsh prophet. Often identified with Aurelius Ambrosius (aka Aurelianus) or with Merlin.
Erinyes	Air-in-yees	Greek Ἐρινύες "Furies" Divine punishers of oath-breakers.

Eumenides	You-men-i-dees	Greek. Εὐμενίδες "Kindly Ones" Euphemistic alternate name for the Erinyes.
Falȝaz	Fal-yaz	Son of Alβiz. Founder of Falias, one of the four great cities of the Tuatha de Dannan
Fenrir	Fen-rear	Norse. "Fen Dweller" A giant wolf. Son of Loki.
Fenrisulfr	Fen-riss-ulf	Norse. "Fenrir Wolf" Alternate name for Fenrir.
Fensalir	Fen-sal-ear	Norse. Dwelling place of Frigg
Fimbulvetr	Fim-Bull-Vetur	Norse. "Great Winter" The long winter that precedes Ragnarok.
Findȝaz	Finth-yaz ("th" as in this)	Son of Alβiz. Founder of Findias, one of the four great cities of the Tuatha de Dannan

Fólkvangr	Folk-vang	Norse. "People-Field" or "Field of Hosts" Freyja's domain where is gathered half of the battle-slain (presumably the half that doesn't go to Valhalla) to train for Ragnarok.
Freyja	Fray-yah	Norse. "The Lady" A Vanir Goddess. Daughter of Njörðr, sister of Freyr, and wife of Óðr.
Freyr	Fray	Norse. "Lord" Brother of Freyja. King of Álfheimr.
Frigg	Frig	Norse. Goddess of Wisdom and foresight. Wife of Odin.
Gaia	Guy-ya	Greek Γαῖα "Earth" or "Land" Mother Goddess. Mother and Mate of Uranus. Mother of the Titans and Kyklopes.

Garmr	Garm	Norse. "Rag" Hel's wolf that guards the gates of Éljúðnir.
Gersemi	G-sem-ee	Norse. Daughter of Freyja
Ginnungagap	Gin-nung-a-gap	Norse. "Yawning Abyss" The primordial void.
Gjallarhorn	Gyal-lar-horn	Norse. "Hollering Horn" The Horn of Heimdallr
Glaðsheimr	Glath-Shaym ("th" as in this)	Norse. "Bright Home" Meeting hall where the Æsir held court. Located in Iðavöllr in Asgard. Valhalla may be located within this great hall.
Gleipnir	Glayp-near	Norse. "Open One" The binding created by the Dvergar to bind Fenrir.
Gorʒaz	Gore-yaz	Son of Alβiz. Founder of Gorias, one of the four great cities of the Tuatha de Dannan
Grimnir	Grim-near	Norse. "Masked One" Alias of Odin

Gungnir	Goong-near	Norse. "Swaying One" Odin's spear.
Gwenddoleu	Goo-en-tho-le-oo	Welsh. King of Arfderydd. Patron of Myrddin
Gwendydd	Goo-en-dith ("th" as in this)	Welsh. Wife of Rydderch. Daughter of Madog Morfryn. Twin sister of Myrddin
Gwion Bach	Goo-ee-on Bach	Welsh. Servant of Ceridwen. Reborn as Taliesin
Gwrtheyrn	Goor-the-urn	Welsh. Vortigern
Gwyddno Garahir	Goo-ith-no Gar-a-hear	Welsh. King of Cantre'r Gwaelod
Gwyn	Goo-in	Welsh. "White" King of Annwn
Gwynedd	Goo-in-eth ("th" as in this)	Welsh. An early Welsh kingdom. Ruled at one time by Math fab Mathonwy
Hati	Hat-ee	Norse. "Hated One" Wolf (or warg) son of Fenrir. Chases Mani across the night sky and will kill him during Ragnarok.
Heimdallr	Haym-dahl	Norse. The watchman of the Gods

Hel	Hell	Norse. Goddess of the Dead. Daughter of Loki. Also the name of the realm of the dead.
Himinbjörg	Him-in-b'yorg	Norse. "Heaven's Castle" Heimdallr's home.
Hnoss	Huh-noss	Norse. Daughter of Freyja
Hoddmimis Holt	Hod-me-mees Holt	Norse. "Mimir's Hoard" location where Líf and Lífþrasir survive Ragnarok.
Hoðr	Hah-th ("th" as in this)	Norse. Murderer of Baldr.
Hrym	Hr-im	Norse. Leader of the Jotnar during Ragnarok.
Huginn	Hoo-gin	Norse. "Thought" One of Odin's two ravens, who fly all over the world to gather information for him.
Hvergelmir	Hv-ergel-meer	Norse. "Bubbling Spring" A major spring located in Niflheimr
Iðavöllr	Ith-a-vaul ("th" as in this)	Norse. "Splendor plain" A meeting place of the gods.

Jarnviðr	Yarn-vith ("th" as in this)	Norse. "Iron Woods" Home of Fenrir's children.
Jólfaðr	Y'all-fah-thar ("th" as in this)	Norse. "Yule Father" Another name for Odin
Jorð	Yorth ("th" as in this)	Norse. "Earth" Earth Mother. Mother of Þorr.
Jormungandr	Your-moon-gand	Norse. "Huge Monster" The Miðgarðsormr (The Midgard Serpent). Son of Loki.
Jotnar	Yote-Nar	Norse. "Powerful Ones" or "Gluttonous Ones" Often translated, somewhat questionably, as Giants.
Jötunheimr	Yotun-haym	Norse. "Jotun Home" Realm of the Jotnar.
Jotunn	Yote-un	Norse. Singular form of Jotnar.
Kronos	Kron-os	Greek. Κρόνος. "The Cutter" Son of Uranus and Gaia. King of the Titans. Note: Not the same figure as Chronos (Χρόνος) "Time"

Kvasir	K-vas-ear	Norse. A God created from the spittle of all the Æsir and Vanir. Killed by the Dvergar Fjalar and Galar, drained of blood and brewed into Odin's Mead of Poetry (See Óðrœrir)
Kyklopes	Ky-klop-ees	Greek. Κύκλωπες "Round-Eyes" or "Circle Eyes" Three one-eyed offspring of Uranus and Gaia, who crafted Zeus' thunderbolt
Langbarðr	Lang-barth ("th" as in this)	Norse. "Long Bearded" Another name for Odin
Laufey	Lau-fee	Norse. "Leafy" Jotun. Mother of Loki
Llallwgan	Hla-hloo-gan	Welsh. "Little Twin" Gwendydd's nickname for Myrddin
Llefelys	H-lev-elis	Welsh. Brother of King Lludd
Lleu	H-lew	Welsh "light" Nephew of King Math of Gwynedd

Lludd	H-looth ("th" as in this)	Welsh. King of Britain. Son of Beli Mawr.
Lóðurr	Low-thur ("th" as in this)	Norse. God who helped Odin animate Ask and Embla. Possible alternate name for Loki, Vili, or Ve.
Loki	Low-Key	Norse. Jotunn. Trickster God. Blood Brother of Odin.
Loptr	Lof-tur	Norse. "Air" Alternate name for Loki.
Madog Morfryn	Ma-doc Mor-vrin	Welsh. "Sea-Crow" Father of Myrddin Wyllt and Gwendydd
Manannan	mah-nuh-nahn	Irish Gaelic. Son of Ler. A God of the Sea and the Otherworld. Possibly related to Manawydan fab Llyr
Manawydan	Man-ah-wu-dan	Welsh. Son of Llŷr. Brother of Brân and Brânwen
Mani	Man-ee	Norse. "Moon" God of the Moon.

Math	Math ("th" as in Thor)	Welsh. King of Gwynedd. Son of Mathonwy. Brother of Dôn.
Mathonwy	Math-on-oo-ee ("th" as in Thor)	Welsh. Father of Dôn and Math
Metis	Mi-tiss	Greek Μῆτις "Wisdom" Titaness. Daughter of Okeanus. Helped Zeus poison Kronos. Mother of Athena.
Miðgarð	Mith-garth ("th" as in this)	Norse. Middle-Garden. Home of mankind. Midgard.
Mimir	Mee-mere	Norse. God of wisdom. Odin sacrificed his eye to Mimir's well for the gift of wisdom.
Mjolnir	M-yole-near	Norse. "Grinder" Þorr's hammer
Móðir Jorð	Mu-theer Yorth ("th" as in this.	Norse. "Mother Earth" Alternate name for Jorð.
Móðsognir	Moeth-sog-near ("th" as in this)	Norse "He Who Drinks in Might" Dvergar King.

Muninn	Moo-nin	Norse. "Memory" One of Odin's two ravens, who fly all over the world to gather information for him.
Murȝaz	Mer-yaz	Son of Alβiz. Founder of Murias, one of the four great cities of the Tuatha de Dannan
Muspelheim	Moo-spell-haym	Norse. "Fire Home" Home of Surtr
Myrddin Wyllt	Mur-thin Wu-hlt	Welsh. 6th Century Welsh bard and prophet. Son of Madog Morfryn. Brother of Gwendydd.
Myrkheim	Merk-haym	Norse. "Darkness Home" Another name for Niðavellir. Home of the Dvergar (Dwarves).
Nemed	Nev-adh	Irish Gaelic. "Holy" Early ruler of Ireland

Niðavellir	Nith-a-vel-lear	Norse. "Dark Fields," aka Myrkheim "Home of Darkness." Home of the Dvergar
Níðhǫggr	Nith-hog	Norse. "Malice Striker" A great serpent that lives in the roots of Yggdrasil.
Niflheim	Niff-el-haym	Norse. "Mist Home" One of the primordial worlds.
Niflhel	Niff-el-hell	Norse. "Misty Hel" Home of Hel. Either a misty region at the lowest level of Hel, or a region in Niflheim in which Hel is located.
Níu Heimar	Ny-ew Haym-ar	Norse. "Nine Homes" or "Nine Worlds" The Norse Cosmos.
Njörðr	Nigh-orth ("th" as in this)	Norse. A Vanir. Father of Freyr and Freyja.
Norðri	Nor-three ("th" as in this)	Norse. "North" One of four Dvergar who hold up the sky.

Nudd	Nooth ("th" as in this)	Welsh. Son of Beli. Early King of Britain
Oðinn	Oh-thin ("th" as in this)	Norse. Odin. Ruler of the gods. Son of Borr and Bestla.
Óðr	Oh-ther ("th" as in this)	Norse. Husband of Freyja.
Óðrœrir	Oh-thur-or-ear ("th" as in this)	Norse. "Stirrer of Inspiration" Odin's Mead of Poetry (or one of its containers). Brewed by Dvergar from the body of Kvasir.
Oisin	Uh-sheen	Irish Gaelic "Young Deer" Irish poet and warrior of the Fianna. Son of Fionn mac Cumhaill and of Sadhbh. Fell in love with Niaṁ Cinn-Óir of Tir na Nog.
Othrys	Oh-thriss ("th" as in Thor)	Greek Ὄθρυς. "Brow" Mountain from which Kronos ruled the Titans.
Ouranos	Our-eh-nos	Greek. Οὐρανός "Rain Maker" Alternate form of Uranus.

Pontos	Pawn-tos	Greek. Πόντος "The Sea" Pre-Olympian sea-god. Son of Gaia.
Prydein	Pru-den	Welsh. Old name for Britain.
Pryderi	Pru-deri	Welsh. King of Dyfed. Son of Pwyll
Prydwen	Prud-oo-en	Welsh "Fair Face" King Arthur's ship.
Pythia	Pie-Thee-uh ("th" as in Thor)	Greek Πυθία High Priestess of Apollo and Oracle of Delphi.
Ragnarök	Rag-na-rock	Norse. "Death of the Gods" The prophesied end of the world.
Renos	Rey-nos	Gaulish. River God. The Rhein river is named for him.
Rhea	Ray-uh	Greek Ῥέα "Ground" or "Earth" (maybe). Daughter of Gaia and Uranus. Sister and wife of Kronos. Mother of Zeus.
Rhun	Roon	Alfar name for the Rhine river.

Rhydderch	Ruth-erkh ("th" as in this)	Welsh. King of Strathclyde. Husband of Gwendydd
Rindr	Rind (rhymes with "wind")	Norse. Mother of Váli by Odin.
Rodonos	Row-doe-nos	Gaulish. River God. The Rhône river is named for him.
Sídhe	Shee	Irish Gaelic "Hill" Cairns. Burial Mounds. Fairy Mounds. The hollow hills of Ireland, where the gods (i.e. The Tuatha De Dannan) retreated to after the coming of men (The Milesians) to Ireland. Possibly gateways to the Otherworld.
Sif	"i" as in if	Norse. "Wife" Wife of Þorr
Sigyn	See-gin ("g" as in gun)	Norse. "victorious girl-friend" Wife of Loki.
Skaði	Ska-thi ("th" as in this)	Norse. Wife of Njörðr.

Skoll	Skole (Rhymes with "toll")	Norse. "Treachery" Wolf son of Fenrir. Chases Sol across the sky and will kill her during Ragnarok.
Sleipnir	Slayp-near	Norse. "The Slipper" Odin's eight-legged horse. Son of Loki, who is the horse's mother.
Sol	Soul	Norse. The Goddess of the Sun
Suðri	Su-three ("th" as in this)	Norse. "South" One of four Dvergar who hold up the sky.
Surtr	Surt	Norse. "Swarthy One" A Jotun who will burn the world during Ragnarok.
Svartalfar	Svart-alf-ar	Norse. "Black Elves" May be another name for Dvergar.
Svartalfheimr	Svart-alf-haym	Norse. "Black-Elf Home" Realm of the Svartalfar, who may or may not be Dvergar by another name.

Taliesin	Tal-ee-ES-in	Welsh "Shining Brow" 6th Century Welsh Bard. He is said to be the reincarnation of Gwion Bach, servant of Ceridwen.
Þorr	Thor ("th" as in Thor)	Norse. "Thunder" Thor, God of Thunder. Son of Oðinn and Jorð. Husband of Sif.
Þrúðr	Thru-thar (First "th" as in Thor, Second "th" as in this)	Norse. "Strength" Daughter of Þorr and Sif. A Valkyrie.
Þunraz	Thun-rahz ("th" as in Thor)	Proto-Germanic. "Thunder" Possible early name for Þorr
Þurisaz	Thur-i-saz ("th" as in Thor)	Brother of Alßiz. Father of the Jotnar.
Tir na nOg	Tear-nah-nowg	Irish Gaelic "Land of the Young" Another name for the Otherworld.
Tiw	Two	Old English. Tyr.

Tiwaz	Two-az	Proto-Germanic. "Day-light sky" An Early name for Tyr, derived from the Proto-Indo European Dyeus.
Tuisto	Two-is-toe	Germanic. Ancestor god to the Germanic tribes, according to Tacitus. Thought to be etymologically connected to Tiwaz, Tiw, and Tvastr.
Tvaṣṭṛ	T-vast-ar	Sanskrit. Vedic artisan god. Thought to be etymologically related to Tiwaz.
Twerg	Tw-erg (One Syllable)	Old High German. Dverg
Twerias	Twer-ee-az	Underground Dvergar city located in Niðavellir
Tylwyth Teg	Tu-loo-ith Teg ("th" as in Thor)	Welsh. "Fair Family"
Tyr	Tear	Norse. God of War. Had one hand bitten off by Fenrir.

Uonaidh	Oon-ayth ("th" as in this)	Gaelic. Ancient Fay Queen
Uranus	Your-eh-nus	Greek. Οὐρανός "Rain Maker" Offspring and mate of Gaia and father of the Titans. May also be the son of Aether
Valhalla	Val-hah-lah	Norse. "Hall of the Slain" Odin's hall where his chosen dead, those deemed worthy by the Valkyries after falling in battle, wait and train for Ragnarok.
Váli	Val-ee	Norse. Son of Odin and Rindr.
Valkyrie	Val-kee-ree	Norse. "Chooser of the Slain"
Vanaheimr	Vana-haym	Norse. "Vanir Home" Realm of the Vanir, a tribe of gods.
Vandar	Van-dar	Alternate name of βanðr Derkaz
Vanir	Van-ear	Norse. A tribe of gods.
Ve	Vay	Norse. Brother of Odin and Vili. Son of Borr and Bestla.

Vestri	Ves-tree	Norse. "West" One of four Dvergar who hold up the sky.
Viðarr	Vith-are ("th" as in this)	Norse. "Wide Ruler" Son of Odin
Vigriðr	Vig-rith ("th" as in this)	Norse. "Battle Surge" Field where Surtr's forces gather for Ragnarok.
Vili	Vi-lee	Norse. Brother of Odin and Ve. Son of Borr and Bestla.
Vortigern	Vort-i-gern	Welsh. King of Britain.
Wīhą	Why-ha	Proto-Germanic form of Ve
Wiljô	Wil-yo	Proto-Germanic form of Vili
Woðanaz	Wo-than-oz ("th" as in this)	Indo-European. Conjectural early name for Odin/Woden
Woden	Woah-den	Old English. Odin
Worsanós	War-sah-nos	Proto-Greek Ϝορσανός "Rain Maker" Early form of Ouranos.
Yggdrasil	Eeg-drass-ill	Norse. "Ygg's Horse." The World Tree. Ygg is possibly another name for Odin.

Ymir	Eye-Mir	Norse. Primordial frost giant. Ancestor of the Jotnar.
Zeus	Ze-oos / Zoos	Greek Ζεύς "Sky" Son of Kronos and Rhea. King of the Gods. See also: Dyeus.
βanðr Derkaz	Van-thar Der-Khaz ("th" as in this)	βanðr the Dark One. Brother of Alβiz. Father of the Dokkalfar.
βanʒuz	Van-yuz	Daughter of Alβiz. Founded the city of Vanias. Vanaheim is named after her.
βurista	Vur-ist-ah	Alfar city founded by βanðr Derkaz and named for his son, βuristiz.
βuristiz	Vur-ist-iz	Son of βanðr Derkaz.

Appendix II: Suggested Further Reading

This list is far from comprehensive and merely represents some of my personal recommendations

General Mythology

Who's Who – Non-Classical Mythology by Egerton Sykes. Awkwardly titled, but an excellent reference book that carries information on world mythologies, including Norse and Celtic myths.

A Dictionary of Creation Myths by David Leeming with Margaret Leeming

Norse Mythology:
Books:

The Poetic Edda (aka The Elder Edda) – One of two major sources for Norse Mythology. There are many translations available. I personally am fond of the version by Henry A Bellows, though some may find his language a little archaic. A free on-line version, which can be downloaded in various eBook formats can be found at WikiSource:
https://en.wikisource.org/wiki/Poetic_Edda

The Prose Edda (aka The Younger Edda) by Snorri Sturluson. This is the second major source for Norse Mythology. It was compiled by Sturluson sometime in the 13th century. As with the Poetic Edda, there are many translations. A free eBook version is available from Project Gutenberg:
http://www.gutenberg.org/ebooks/18947

Norse Mythology by Neil Gaiman.

Websites:
Nordic Culture (https://norse-mythology.net/) An site with an excellent overview of Norse Mythology, Norse Sagas, and the Vikings.
Timeless Myths: Norse Mythology (https://www.timelessmyths.com/norse/index.html) Another good site with an overview of Norse Mythology, including genealogical tables.

Celtic Mythology (Including Arthurian Legends)
Books:
The Mabinogion. Easily the most important collection of Welsh myth and legend. I highly recommend the recent translation by Sioned Davies. The seminal translation by Lady Charlotte Guest is available as a free eBook from Project Gutenberg (http://www.gutenberg.org/ebooks/5160)
The Book of Taliesin translated by Rowan Williams and Gwyneth Lewis. A wonderful new English translation of one of the greatest collections of medieval Welsh poetry.
The History of the Kings of Britain by Geoffrey of Monmouth.
The Life of Merlin (Vita Merlini) by Geoffrey of Monmouth. The story of Myrddin Wyllt, whom Geoffrey had used to create the figure of Merlin in his History. This represents the more traditional Welsh view of Myrddin/Merlin, though Geoffrey tries to reconcile the Welsh legends with his almost entirely imaginary Arthurian wizard. I highly recommend the recent verse translation by Mark Walker.

Scotland's Merlin by Tim Clarkson. A very thorough study of the legend of Merlin/Myrddin.

Lebor Gabála Érenn (The Book of Invasions of Ireland) translated by R. A. S. Macalister. The core of the Irish Mythological Cycle. So far as I know the book is out of print and fairly hard to find, but the contents can be found on Mary Jones' Celtic Literature Collective (http://www.maryjones.us/ctexts/leborgabala.html)

Dictionary of Celtic Mythology by Peter Berresford Ellis

Dictionary of Irish Mythology by Peter Berresford Ellis

The Encyclopedia of Arthurian Legends by Ronan Coghlan. Easily the best reference book on Arthuriana.

Websites:

Mary Jones' Celtic Literature Collective (http://www.maryjones.us/ctexts/index.html) A marvelous collection of Celtic texts, including many of the ones mentioned above. Contains many texts that are not easily available anywhere else.

Mary Jones' Celtic Encyclopedia (http://www.maryjones.us/jce/jce_index.html) An excellent online reference for Celtic myth and culture.

Timeless Myths: Celtic Mythology (https://www.timelessmyths.com/celtic/index.html) A good overview of Celtic Mythology (both Welsh and Irish). Includes genealogical tables.

Timeless Myths: Arthurian Legends

(https://www.timelessmyths.com/arthurian/index.html)

Classical Mythology
Books:
Who's Who – Classical Mythology by Michael Grant and John Hazel. And indispensable reference for every figure in Classical Mythology

Mythology: Timeless Tales of Gods and Heroes by Edith Hamilton. Written in the 1940s, but still one of the best introductions to Classical Mythology.

Websites:
Timeless Myths: Classical Mythology (https://www.timelessmyths.com/classical/index.html) A good overview of Classical Mythology.

ACKNOWLEDGMENTS

First, I'd like to say a very big "Thank you!" to everyone who bought, read, and reviewed my first poetry collection, *The Darkness of His Dreams*. Every sale of that book meant more to me than I can say.

This collection had its seed planted in 2016 when I posted a few poems on my blog that concerned Norse Myths. They had been written purely for my own amusement, but I was pleasantly surprised by the positive feedback I received, which encouraged me to write more mythologically inspired poems, which led directly to the conception of the present volume. I am grateful to all those who commented on those pieces and encouraged me to write more.

Special thanks to the talented Kindra M Austin, a good friend who graciously read a few of my works in progress to give me advice and encouragement. Kindra is a talented writer, a thoughtful editor, and a good friend.

Thank you to Kristiana Reed, poet and editor of *Free Verse Revolution*, where the first version of 'At the Beginning' was published, based on a prompt by Kristiana.

Thank you to *The Ink Owl*, where the original version of 'Twilight Visions' first appeared.

Thank you to Rachel "Quirky" Schenk for a well-timed, unexpectedly inspiring, Tarot card reading via Zoom, which occurred during the final editing of this book.

And, as always, thank you, Mom & Dad. I miss you.

ABOUT THE AUTHOR

John W. Leys is an indie-poet who lives in Albany, Oregon with his chihuahua, Cosmo. He's been writing poetry since he was 14 and has been fascinated with mythology for even longer. He served five years in the US Army, has a BA in  Religious Studies from the University of South Florida, and studied for his MA in Judaic Studies at the Graduate School of the Jewish Theological Seminary. His first poetry collection, *The Darkness of His Dreams,* was published in 2019.

When not writing poetry, John is usually playing one of his many ukuleles or reading ancient Hellenistic philosophy for fun.

JohnWLeys.com

linktr.ee/johnwleys

www.ingramcontent.com/pod-product-compliance
Lightning Source LLC
Chambersburg PA
CBHW071351080526
44587CB00017B/3051